Suffering from

Guilt

By Debra Mathers

Edited by Thomas J. Doyle

Publishing House
St. Louis

Editorial assistant: Phoebe Wellman

Unless otherwise stated, Scripture taken from the Holy Bible, New International Version®. Copyright © 1973, 1978, 1984 by International Bible Society. Used by permission of Zondervan Publishing House. All rights reserved.

The "NIV" and "New International Version" trademarks are registered in the United States Patent and Trademark Office by International Bible Society. Use of either trademark requires the permission of International Bible Society.

Scripture quotations marked NASB are from the NEW AMERICAN STANDARD BIBLE, © The Lockman Foundation 1960, 1962, 1963, 1968, 1971, 1972, 1973, 1975, 1977, and are used by permission.

Copyright © 1993 Concordia Publishing House
3558 S. Jefferson Avenue, St. Louis, MO 63118-3968
Manufactured in the United States of America

1 2 3 4 5 6 7 8 9 10   02 01 00 99 98 97 96 95 94 93

Contents

❖

Guilt and Joe Christian

Focusing Our Sights

Jesus died on a cross for you 2,000 years ago. What have you done for Him today?

As fallen human beings, we are guilty; we fail to follow God in every area of our lives. Sometimes we attempt to use guilt to motivate others by holding up a model of a Christian ideal. But motivating in this way can lead to either self-righteousness or despair rather than the desired spiritual growth. We do not need to live lives that are controlled by guilt. Through Jesus' perfect life and gruesome death, God provided the one-time sacrifice to forgive our sins, take away our guilt, bring us into fellowship with Him forever, and give us freedom to follow as He leads.

Focusing Our Attention

Guilt takes many forms in our lives. We feel guilty, and rightly so, when we have done something wrong. This kind of guilt leads us to seek God's forgiveness and the forgiveness of those we may have hurt. Guilt can also arise from feelings of inadequacy, of not living up to the expectations others and/or God have for us. Read the following articles. See if you can spot any hidden, or not so hidden, guilt inducers.

Countdown . . .

Ten little church members came to worship all the time. One fell out with the pastor, and then there were nine.

Nine little members stayed up late. One overslept and then there were eight.

Eight church members on their way to heaven. One took the low road and now there are seven.

Seven church members all chirping like chicks. One didn't like the music, and now there are six.

Six church members seemed very much alive, but one got the itch to travel, and this left five.

Five church members pulling for heaven's shore. One tired and got disgruntled, and this left four.

Four church members, busy as can be, but one got his feelings hurt, and now there are three.

Three church members and the story's almost done, for two of them got weary and this left one . . .

Two church members each won one more. Now don't you see? 2 + 2 = 4!

Four church members worked early and late. Each one brought one and now there are eight.

Have you got the message, pointed and true? Come on folks, we've got a job to do. For you see, these eight church members, if they double as before, in just seven weeks would have 1024!

In this little jingle there is a lesson true. You belong to one of the two—either the *building* or the *wrecking* crew!

Life of a One-Dollar Bill

Two old bills were about to be destroyed; a one-dollar bill and a twenty-dollar bill.

The $1 bill said to the $20 bill, "What was your life like?"

The $20 bill answered, "Oh, just wonderful. Why, I have been in the best restaurants, boutiques, and hotels. I went to Europe three times! What was your life like, $1 bill?"

The $1 bill sighed, "Same old thing . . . went to church . . . went to church . . . went to church."

Just Suppose . . .

❑ that you had to run for church membership as a candidate runs for political office—would you win or lose?

❑ that membership was good for one year only and that reelection depended upon your participation during that time— would you be reinstated or would you be dropped?

❑ that there was a long list of people waiting to get in—would you be more alive to your duty as a member of this organization?

❑ that you were called upon to explain why we should keep your name on the rolls—have you a case to offer in your defense?

❑ that every member of this organization did as much for it as you are doing—would

7

❖

more seats be needed, or would the doors be shut?

Complete the chart on the following page. List the guilt inducers found in "Countdown . . .," "Life of a One-Dollar Bill," and "Just Suppose."

Focusing on the Issue

1. Suppose the people who promoted the views mentioned in the articles were given the opportunity to construct a person who would fulfill their requirements. Describe this person.

2. When people are confronted with statements of this sort, they respond in various ways. How well did you measure up to these statements? Place an *X* next to the statement that best describes your feelings.

_____ Sure, I fall short on a few of them, but my strengths more than make up for my failures.

_____ Not only do I fail to measure up, but I now feel guilty for not doing better.

What is the danger with each of these statements? How could both of these statements damage your relationship with God?

Countdown . . .	Life of a One-Dollar Bill	Just Suppose . . .

❖

3. People suffering from spiritual guilt may feel like the members pictured in the cartoon. Why?

4. What positive results can come from using guilt to motivate people?

5. What negative consequences come from using guilt to motivate people?

Focusing on God's Word

It is likely that there will always be people who establish rules for how people should or should not behave. Sometimes we will respond to these injunctions with guilt and repentance and sometimes we will respond with pride and arrogance. The only certainty is that we are unable to meet perfectly the expectations God or people establish for us.

❖❖❖❖❖❖❖❖❖❖❖❖❖❖❖❖❖❖❖❖❖❖❖❖❖

"The law is only a shadow of the good things that are coming—not the realities themselves. For this reason it can never, by the same sacrifices repeated endlessly year after year, make perfect those who draw near to worship. If it could, would they not have stopped being offered? For the worshipers would have been cleansed once for all, and would no longer have felt guilty for their sins." (Hebrews 10:1–2)

❖❖❖❖❖❖❖❖❖❖❖❖❖❖❖❖❖❖❖❖❖❖❖❖❖

1. Before Jesus came, God instituted sacrifice as a way to deal with people's sin and guilt. Underline the words that describe the effectiveness of these sacrifices at removing the load of guilt from people burdened with sin.

2. The sacrifices prescribed by the law are described as a shadow of the good things that are coming. Later in **Hebrews 10** the author describes "the good things that are coming." Read **Hebrews 10:12** and circle the words that describe the effectiveness of this "good thing."

❖❖❖❖❖❖❖❖❖❖❖❖❖❖❖❖❖❖❖❖❖❖❖❖❖

"But when this priest [Jesus] had offered for all time one sacrifice for sins, He sat down at the right hand of God." (Hebrews 10:12)

❖❖❖❖❖❖❖❖❖❖❖❖❖❖❖❖❖❖❖❖❖❖❖❖❖

❖

3. Describe in your own words the one-time sacrifice of Jesus.

4. A famous God-is-dead theologian, when asked "What do you mean by God?" replied, "God? God, to me, is that little inner voice that always says 'That's not quite good enough'." (Reprinted from *Healing for Damaged Emotions,* by David A. Seamands, published by Victor Books, Copyright © 1981, SP Publications, Inc., Wheaton, IL 60187.) Yet **John 3:17** tells us that God did not send Jesus to condemn the world but to save the world.

Sometimes we don't recognize who is accusing us, making us feel guilty for past sins—sins forgiven by the "one time sacrifice" of Jesus. **Revelation 12:10** says, "Now the salvation, and the power, and the kingdom of our God and the authority of His Christ have come, for the accuser of our brethren has been thrown down, who accuses them before our God day and night" (NASB). If Jesus is not accusing us or condemning us, who is, according to this passage? What are some ways he accuses or condemns us?

❖

5. What does **Jeremiah 29:11,** "For I know the plans I have for you," declares the Lord, "plans to prosper you and not to harm you, plans to give you hope and a future," teach us about God's desire for us?

Focusing on My Life

1. Check all of the things the accuser Satan might cause you to believe to make you feel guilty.

_____ My sins are too great for Jesus to forgive.

_____ God could never love me.

_____ If I could only do better, God would love me more.

_____ I could never be as good a Christian as . . .

2. Going around the room, say the following to the person sitting on your left, filling his or her name in the blank.

_____ ,
Jesus' death on the cross has gained forgiveness for all your sins. You stand guilt-free before God. You are His workmanship, created in Christ Jesus for good works which God has prepared beforehand for you to walk in. Go in peace.

13

Focusing on the Week Ahead

1. Look for guilt inducers and examine how they make you feel.

2. Write the following promises from God's Word on index cards: **Revelation 12:10; Jeremiah 29:11; John 3:16–17; Psalm 103:12; Ephesians 2:8–10.** Carry one or more in a pocket, purse, wallet, or briefcase. Or hang them around your home or at your place of work. Read them when you feel guilty for not living up to other's expectations or God's expectation, or when guilt over past and forgiven sins surfaces.

❖

Guilt—Can't Live with It, Can't Live without It

Focusing Our Sights

If guilt can be misused by ourselves and by others who want to control us, why not get rid of it, decide it doesn't exist anymore? Some secular writers have advocated just that. Retrain your conscience so you no longer feel guilt or use the guilt to motivate yourself to become a better human being. Is eliminating guilt the best way to deal with it? Or can guilt serve a useful purpose in our lives?

Focusing Our Attention

Guilt can be like extra weight—something we drag around with us to slow our pace and hamper our agility. Just about every role we have in life has the potential to cause guilt when we don't measure up to the standards we have set for ourselves or for others. In the past few years we've heard about working mother guilt, absent father guilt, aging parent guilt, and more.

1. Jot down times in your life when you have struggled with guilt. Consider each of the expectations each of the following have of you: your children, parents, employer, church, government, and God.

2. What about personal guilt? List some expectations that you don't, can't, or won't live up to?

Focusing on the Issue

What to do with the problem of guilt?

People usually deal with guilt in four ways:
- Deny its existence.
- Accept guilt and use it to become the persons they have always wanted to be.
- Bear the guilt and drag it around wherever they go.
- Dump the guilt onto the nearest person.

Each of the following quotes lists one of the four ways people handle guilt.

1. "At the congressional Iran-Contra hearings there was a repeating theme: high officials of the government expressing a self-righteous commitment to flaunting the laws. What impressed this viewer most of all was simply the fact that the culprits had made up their minds not to feel bad!" (From *What's So Bad About Guilt?* Copyright © by Harlan J. Wechsler, Ph. D. Reprinted by permission of Simon and Shuster, Inc.)

React to this statement: If I don't acknowledge my guilt, it doesn't exist.

2. "Don't undersell guilt. While it certainly inhibits good feelings, it is also a catalyst that enables those good feelings to grow. Guilt can be a motivational force that is hard to beat — if it is used well." (From *What's So Bad About Guilt?* Copyright © by Harlan J. Wechsler, Ph. D. Reprinted by permission of Simon and Shuster, Inc.)

React to this statement: There is nothing wrong with using guilt to obtain desirable behavior from others. The world is a better place because of it.

3. "He had never been able to forgive himself. He had sought God's forgiveness, and with his head, believed he had it. But the guilt still plagued him and he hated himself. Every time he looked in the mirror, he couldn't stand what he was seeing." (Reprinted from *Healing for Damaged Emotions* by David A. Seamands, published by Victor Books, Copyright © 1981, SP Publications, Inc., Wheaton, IL 60187.)

React to this statement: We should bear the pain of our guilt and sins. After all, we are the ones who cause it.

❖

4. "In March 1978 a Colorado man brought a malparenting suit against his mother and father. He sued them for $300,000 for lousing up his life, claiming they had intentionally done a terrible job of parenting and had made him what he was." (Reprinted from *Putting Away Childish Things* by David A. Seamands, published by Victor Books, copyright © 1982, SP Publications, Inc., Wheaton, IL 60187.)

React to this statement: It's okay to transfer our guilt to others, by blaming them for our behavior.

Focusing on God's Word

"As it is, however, the sacrifices serve year after year to remind people of their sins. For the blood of bulls and goats can never take away sins" (**Hebrews 10:3,4** TEV).

"Day after day every priest stands and performs his religious duties; again and again he offers the same sacrifices, which can never take away sins" (**Hebrews 10:11**).

1. In the Old Testament the yearly sacrifices reminded the people of the guilt of their sins, and their need for forgiveness. The sacrifices never took away sins—a permanent solution was needed. "But God demonstrates His own love for us in this: While we were still sinners, Christ died for us" (**Romans 5:8**). How did Jesus Christ become our "once for all" sacrifice for sins?

2. Corrie ten Boom, a woman imprisoned in a concentration camp for hiding and rescuing Jews during the Second World War, once stated: "Guilt never heals; its purpose is only to lead us to the Healer."

How is this the most effective way to deal with our guilt?

3. (Romans 3:23): "For all have sinned and fall short of the glory of God." Compare this verse to the statement "If I don't acknowledge my guilt, it doesn't exist."

4. "There is nothing wrong with using guilt to obtain desirable behavior from others. The world is a better place because of it" is an argument used to justify the use of guilt. How does this statement compare to "Therefore, there is now no condemnation for those who are in Christ Jesus, because through Christ Jesus the law of the Spirit of life set me free from the law of sin and death" **(Romans 8:1–2)?**

5. "We should bear the pain of our guilt and sins. After all, we are the ones who cause it." How does **1 John 1:9** compare: "If we confess our sins, He is faithful and just and will forgive us our sins and purify us from all unrighteousness" answer this point of view?

6. Jesus said "Do not judge, and you will not be judged. Do not condemn, and you will not be condemned" **(Luke 6:37)**. How do you think Jesus would respond to the statement

❖

"It's okay to transfer our guilt to others, by blaming them for our behavior."

Focusing on My Life

In the chart on the following page, column 1 lists again the four ways that people deal with guilt. In column 2 write an example of when you have dealt with guilt in each of the four ways.Then silently confess to God the inappropriate ways you have dealt with guilt. Allow a partner to assure you of God's grace, reading the following to you:

❖❖❖❖❖❖❖❖❖❖❖❖❖❖❖❖❖❖❖❖❖❖❖❖

In the mercy of almighty God, Jesus Christ was given to die for us, and for His sake God forgives us all our sins. To those who believe in Jesus Christ He gives the power to become the children of God and bestows on them the Holy Spirit. May the Lord, who has begun this good work in us, bring it to completion in the day of our Lord Jesus Christ (LW, p. 159).

❖❖❖❖❖❖❖❖❖❖❖❖❖❖❖❖❖❖❖❖❖❖❖❖

Closing

A closing prayer: Father, we know we are coming into the presence of a God who is consistent and loving. We know that You under-

❖

Ways People Deal with Guilt

1. Deny its existence.

2. Accept guilt and use it to become the persons they have always wanted to be.

3. Bear the guilt and drag it around wherever they go.

4. Dump the guilt onto the nearest person.

Example from My Life

stand how our guilt weighs us down and causes us to seek solutions that are harmful to us. We know that You are very aware of our need for a solution to our guilt. You lovingly sent Jesus to take our need upon Himself by dying on the cross for our sins. You are Immanuel, God with Us, in all that we experience. You invite us to come confidently before You and give You our guilt and our sins, and You promise to cleanse us. Father, for this great gift we praise You. In Jesus' name, Amen.

Focusing on the Week Ahead

Practice taking your guilt to God in prayer. Seek His direction and counsel for each situation.

3 Guilt and the Hardened Heart

Focusing Our Sights

Through Jesus God has provided us freedom—freedom from sin, death, and the power of Satan. He promises to relieve us of our burden of guilt as we confess our sins. God enables us by His Spirit's power to forgive those who have sinned against us.

Focusing Our Attention

At a meeting for sexually abused people, a woman in the audience stood up and said, "I don't go for any talk about forgiveness. I think it is wrong to forgive someone who has sexually abused a child."

React to this woman's statement.

It is hard to forgive when we have done nothing to deserve a wrong committed against us. Corrie ten Boom, a former prisoner in a Nazi concentration camp, described the feelings she had as, years after her release, she met face-to-face one of the former guards of the camp.

It was in a church in Munich that I saw him, a balding heavy-set man in a gray overcoat, a brown felt hat clutched between his hands. People were filing out of the basement room where I had just spoken, moving along the rows of wooden chairs to the door at the rear. It was 1947, and I had come from Holland to defeated Germany with the message that God forgives.

It was the truth they needed most to hear In that bitter, bombed-out land, and I gave them my favorite mental picture. Maybe because the sea is never far from a Hollander's mind, I liked to think that that's where forgiven sins were thrown. "When we confess our sins," I said, "God casts them into the deepest ocean, gone forever."

The solemn faces stared back at me, not quite daring to believe. There were never questions after talks in Germany in 1947. People stood up in silence, in silence collected their wraps, in silence left the room.

And that's when I saw him, working his way forward against the others. One moment I saw the overcoat and the brown hat; the next, a blue uniform and a visored cap with its skull and crossbones. It came back with a rush: the huge room with its harsh overhead lights, the pathetic pile of dresses and shoes in the center of the floor, the shame of walking naked past this man. I could see my sister's frail form ahead of me, ribs sharp beneath the parchment skin. Betsie, how thin you were!

Betsie and I had been arrested for concealing Jews in our home during the Nazi occupation of Holland; this man had been a guard at Ravensbruck concentration camp where we were sent.

Now he was in front of me, hand thrust out: "A fine message, Fräulein! How good it is to know that, as you say, all our sins are at the bottom of the sea!"

And I, who had spoken so glibly of forgiveness, fumbled in my pocketbook rather than take that hand. He would not remember me, of course—how could he remember one prisoner among those thousands of women?

But I remembered him and the leather crop swinging from his belt. It was the first time since my release that I had been face to face with one of my captors and my blood seemed to freeze.

"You mentioned Ravensbruck in your talk," he was saying. "I was a guard in there." No, he did not remember me.

"But since that time," he went on, "I have become a Christian. I know that God has forgiven me for the cruel things I did there, but I would like to hear it from your lips as well. Fräulein—" again the hand came out—"will you forgive me?"

And I stood there—I whose sins had every day to be forgiven—and could not. Betsie had died in that place—could he erase her slow terrible death simply for the asking? (From *I'm Still Learing to Forgive*. Reprinted with permission from *Guideposts Magazine*. Copyright © 1972 By Guideposts Associates, Inc., Carmel, New York 10512.)

❖❖❖❖❖❖❖❖❖❖❖❖❖❖❖❖❖❖❖❖❖❖❖

1. What feelings do you think Corrie ten Boom experienced as she struggled with the man's question, "Will you forgive me?"

2. What feelings do you think the former guard experienced as he asked, "Will you forgive me?"

3. How might you have responded to the former guard?

Focusing on the Issue

1. "To forgive or not to forgive?" That is the question that confronted Corrie ten Boom. How might her decision affect her relationship with
  a. God?

  b. herself?

  c. the former guard?

2. Why do you think the former guard needed to hear, "I forgive you"? How might Carrie's decision affect the former guard?

3. How does her statement "I whose sins had every day to be forgiven" relate to the former guard's sins?

Let's see how she responded.

❖❖❖❖❖❖❖❖❖❖❖❖❖❖❖❖❖❖❖❖❖❖❖❖❖

It could not have been many seconds that he stood there, hand held out, but to me it seemed hours as I wrestled with the most difficult thing I had ever had to do.

For I had to do it—I knew that. The message that God forgives has a prior condition: that we forgive those who have injured us. "If you do not forgive men their trespasses," Jesus says, "neither will your Father in heaven forgive your trespasses."

I knew it not only as a commandment of God, but as a daily experience. Since the end of the war I had had a home in Holland for victims of Nazi brutality. Those who were able to forgive their former enemies were able also

❖

to return to the outside world and rebuild their lives, no matter what the physical scars. Those who nursed bitterness remained invalids. It was as simple and as horrible as that.

And still I stood there with the coldness clutching my heart. But forgiveness is not an emotion—I knew that too. Forgiveness is an act of the will, and the will can function regardless of the temperature of the heart. "Jesus, help me!" I prayed silently. "I can lift my hand. I can do that much. You supply the feeling."

And so woodenly, mechanically, I thrust my hand into the one stretched out to me. And as I did, an incredible thing took place. The current started in my shoulder, raced down my arm, sprang into our joined hands. And then this healing warmth seemed to flood my whole being, bringing tears to my eyes.

"I forgive you, brother!" I cried. "With all my heart!"

For a long moment we grasped each other's hands, the former guard and the former prisoner. I had never known God's love so intensely as I did then. (From *I'm Still Learning to Forgive*. Reprinted with permission from *Guideposts Magazine*. Copyright © 1972 by Guideposts Associates, Inc., Carmel, New York 10512.)

❖❖❖❖❖❖❖❖❖❖❖❖❖❖❖❖❖❖❖❖❖❖❖

4. What did Corrie ten Boom give up, when she chose to forgive the former guard?

5. Who gave her the strength to "forgive us our trespasses as we forgive those who trespass against us?"

6. The former guard knew Jesus had forgiven him and so had Corrie ten Boom. What did the man then need to do to erase his guilt?

Focusing on God's Word

What love God has shown us by providing in Christ the forgiveness for all our sins and, in addition, enabling us to love and forgive one another.

❖❖❖❖❖❖❖❖❖❖❖❖❖❖❖❖❖❖❖❖❖❖❖

Therefore, as God's chosen people, holy and dearly loved, clothe yourselves with compassion, kindness, humility, gentleness and patience. Bear with each other and forgive whatever grievances you may have against one another. Forgive as the Lord forgave you. And over all these virtues put on love, which binds them all together in perfect unity.

Let the peace of Christ rule in your hearts, since as members of one body you were called to peace. And be thankful. Let the word of Christ dwell in you richly as you teach and admonish one another with all wisdom, and as you sing psalms, hymns and spiritual songs with gratitude in your hearts to God. And whatever you do, whether in word or deed, do it all in the name of the Lord Jesus, giving thanks to God the Father through Him. (Colossians 3:12–17)

❖❖❖❖❖❖❖❖❖❖❖❖❖❖❖❖❖❖❖❖❖❖❖❖❖❖

1. Circle the characteristics God's Spirit desires to bring to the lives of His forgiven people as described in the Colossians passage.

2. What does God's forgiveness motivate us to do toward others as the Holy Spirit works within us? Underline these as you find them.

3. Put a box around the phrases beginning with the word *Let* that point to Christ as the source of the power to lead a life of forgiveness.

4. "If we confess our sins, He is faithful and just and will forgive us our sins and purify us from all unrighteousness" **(1 John 1:9).** What does God work in our hearts as we confess our sins to Him?

5. James states that if we "confess our sins to each other and pray for each other . . . [we] will be healed" **(James 5:16)**. How can confessing our sins to each other bring healing?

Focusing on My Life

1. Think of a time when you had difficulty forgiving someone. Write the results of your unforgiveness.

2. Think of a time when you had great difficulty forgiving yourself. Write the consequences of refusing to forgive yourself.

❖

3. Think of a time when God enabled you to forgive someone else or yourself. Write the results.

What will you do the next time you have the opportunity to forgive? are in need of forgiveness? have received the assurance of God's forgiveness through faith in Jesus?

Consider two sponges. One is hard and dried out. The other is soft and moist. Which would you rather use to clean a dirty window? The hard sponge cannot absorb the dirt. The two surfaces will scrape each other. If you take the soft, moist sponge to the dirty window you will find that it has an amazing capacity to absorb the dirt and clean the window. The soft sponge, in effect, takes the dirt from the window upon itself.

4. How does God's love change our hearts?

Pray together,

✦✦✦✦✦✦✦✦✦✦✦✦✦✦✦✦✦✦✦✦✦✦✦✦✦✦✦✦

Father, God,
My eyes are dry
My faith is old
My heart is hard
My prayers are cold
And I know how I ought to be
Alive to You and dead to me

Oh, what can be done
For an old heart like mine
Soften it up with oil and wine
The oil is You, Your Spirit of love
Please wash me anew
In the wine of Your Blood.

✦✦✦✦✦✦✦✦✦✦✦✦✦✦✦✦✦✦✦✦✦✦✦✦✦✦✦✦

In Jesus' name. Amen.

Focusing on the Week Ahead

Do you carry excess baggage, loads of unforgiven sins and guilt over past sins? Consider doing some spring cleaning— confession and absolution. Make an appointment with your pastor to confess your sins and receive personal assurance of God's complete forgiveness for all sins through Jesus' sacrificial death on the cross. Allow the shower of God's love and forgiveness to enable you to forgive those who have hurt you.

❖

Corrie ten Boom tells of a further incident in her life when she had trouble forgetting a situation for which she had forgiven someone. She kept rehashing the incident in her mind. She asked God for help.

❖❖❖❖❖❖❖❖❖❖❖❖❖❖❖❖❖❖❖❖❖❖❖❖❖

His help came in the form of a kindly Lutheran pastor to whom I confessed my failure after two sleepless weeks. "Up in that church tower," he said, nodding out the window, "is a bell which is rung by pulling on a rope. But you know what? After the sexton lets go of the rope, the bell keeps on singing. First ding, then dong. Slower and slower until there's a final dong and it stops. I believe the same thing is true of forgiveness. When we forgive, we take our hand off the rope. But if we've been tugging at our grievances for a long time, we mustn't be surprised if the old angry thoughts keep coming for a while. They're just the ding-dongs of the old bell slowing down."

And so it proved to be. There were a few more midnight reverberations, a couple of dings when the subject came up in my conversations. But the force—which was my willingness in the matter—had gone out of them. They came less and less often and at last stopped altogether. And so I discovered another secret of forgiveness: we can trust God not only above our emotions, but also above our thoughts. (From *I'm Still Learning to Forgive*. Reprinted with permission from *Guideposts Magazine*. Copyright © 1972 by Guideposts Associates, Inc., Carmel, New York 10512.)

❖❖❖❖❖❖❖❖❖❖❖❖❖❖❖❖❖❖❖❖❖❖❖❖❖

Try not to become discouraged if the way seems hard. God is with you and will see you

❖

through. He promises to strengthen you and empower you to forgive as the Holy Spirit works through God's words of forgiveness found in Scripture.

❖

Encouraging One Another—Freedom from Guilt

Focusing Our Sights

When we receive God's love and forgiveness through Jesus, the Holy Spirit cleans out the closet of our old wounds and hurts, freeing us from guilt and enabling us to encourage one another.

Focusing Our Attention

Read aloud the following statements with feeling.

A. To a Son or Daughter

"I thought for sure you would get all A's on your report card."

B. To a Pastor

"There sure weren't very many people in church today."

C. To a Teacher

"My son's last teacher had him so enthused about learning he couldn't wait to come to school."

D. To a Church Member

"I know you worked hard on the fund-raiser. I just can't help wondering what went wrong."

E. To a Parent

"I hate you. You never let me do anything."

Focusing on the Issue

1. What affect do these five statements have on you?

2. How might these statements cause you to feel guilty?

3. Share the most discouraging thing anybody ever said to you.

4. Share the most encouraging thing anybody ever said to you.

5. Compare the feelings you experienced when someone said something discouraging to the feelings you had when you heard something encouraging.

Focusing on God's Word

❖❖❖❖❖❖❖❖❖❖❖❖❖❖❖❖❖❖❖❖❖❖❖❖

Therefore, brothers, since we have confidence to enter the Most Holy Place by the blood of Jesus, by a new and living way opened for us through the curtain, that is, His body, and since we have a great priest over the house of God, let us draw near to God with a sincere heart in full assurance of faith, having our hearts sprinkled to cleanse us from a guilty conscience and having our bodies washed with pure water. Let us hold unswervingly to the hope we profess, for He who promised is faithful. And let us consider how we may spur one another on toward love and

❖

good deeds. Let us not give up meeting together, as some are in the habit of doing, but let us encourage one another—and all the more as you see the Day approaching. (Hebrews 10:19–25)

❖❖❖❖❖❖❖❖❖❖❖❖❖❖❖❖❖❖❖❖❖❖❖❖

1. When Jesus died on the cross the curtain that separated the Holy Place from the Most Holy Place in the temple was torn in two. What did the tearing of the curtain symbolize?

2. Summarize, in your own words, the words missing from the passage below. Try to fit your summary on the lines provided.

Because Jesus shed His blood for us, we can

_____

_____

_____

having our hearts sprinkled to

_____

_____ conscience.

3. Through Jesus' death on the cross we have complete forgiveness. Yes, *complete* forgiveness. No longer do we have to hold onto guilt over past sins. Jesus received the punishment we deserved because of our sins. We receive the reward Jesus' deserved—abundant

❖

life on earth and eternal life with Him in heav-
en. As those whom God has freed from the
chains of guilt, the writer to the Hebrews
encourages us to do five things. List those five
things.

a.

b.

c.

d.

e.

4. Write some discouraging statements
that might torpedo each of the five things.

5. Write a statement that would encourage
others to
a. draw near to God

❖

b. hold to the hope we profess

c. love and do good deeds

d. meet together

Focusing on My Life

1. What happens when discouraging words are spoken to or about
a. family

b. church

c. classroom

d. country

2. What happens when encouraging words are spoken to or about
  a. family

  b. church

  c. classroom

  d. country

3. Romans 15:5–7 says, "May the God who gives endurance and encouragement give you a spirit of unity among yourselves as you follow Christ Jesus, so that with one heart and mouth you may glorify the God and Father of our Lord Jesus Christ.

Accept one another, then, just as Christ accepted you, in order to bring praise to God."

What does this tell us about God's love for us?

4. How can we demonstrate Christ's acceptance of us in our words and actions?

5. How can our acceptance of others transform families, churches, classrooms, and/or countries?

6. "Encourage" means to inspire with courage, spirit, or hope; to hearten (*Webster's New Collegiate Dictionary*).

Write your name at the top of a blank sheet of paper. (If you are alone, list on the paper all the encouraging statements people have said to you over the years.) Pass the sheet around to each member of the group until it returns to you. Your instructions are to hearten the person whose name appears at the top of the sheet by writing a sentence or two of encouragement to them.

7. Pray together: **Father, we end this celebration of discovery and encouragement with praise to You—for Your words, for Your provision for us, for Your Son and for the gift of the Holy Spirit. Father, we have not always been loved, accepted, and encouraged in our lives. Sometimes**

❖

people have spoken very discouraging words to us. Father, help us to forgive them. Also Father, we confess to You that we have not always loved, accepted, and encouraged others as we could have. We thank You that Your Son Jesus has forgiven and made us whole by His death on the cross. Be with us now as we go forward in Your name, strengthened and encouraged, that we might become strengtheners and encouragers. In Your Son's name, with all praise and glory to You, our most high Dad. Amen.

Focusing on the Week Ahead

Think of ways you can encourage or spur on the members of your family, the people you work with, your church family, the people who govern you, all those you come into contact with.

Begin to keep a list of Bible verses you come across or hear that specifically encourage you, hearten you, or spur you on. Refer to them in times of discouragement.

Notes for the Leader

1—Guilt
and Joe Christian

❖ Focusing Our Sights

(About 2 Minutes)
Read aloud and briefly discuss the goal statement.

❖ Focusing Our Attention

(About 5 Minutes)
Ask for volunteers to read aloud the three guilt inducers. Complete the chart. Discuss the guilt inducers.

❖ Focusing on the Issue

(About 10 Minutes)
1. Answers will vary. The person would possibly have the following qualities: nonargumentative, early to bed, sinless, noncritical, not restless, accepting, energetic, not overly sensitive, never tired, hard worker, generous.

2. Answers will vary. Point out that either feeling can be hazardous to our faith. The danger with the first choice is that this attitude can cause us to feel self-righteous, "I'm doing just fine," with little or no need for a Savior. The second choice can cause us to experience unhealthy guilt. Jesus lived a perfect life on our behalf and then died on the cross to secure for us forgiveness of sins and eternal life. When we continue to feel guilt over previously forgiven sins, we fail to acknowledge God's grace and forgiveness. This guilt may cause us to question our faith.

3. After studying the cartoon, discuss the questions that follow. Spiritual guilt leaves a person without hope, questioning the forgiveness Christ has earned, and doubting God's free gift of salvation.

4–5. Guilt is a powerful stimulus. It can change a person's behavior. Unfortunately, it does little to change behaviors for the long term. It most often makes people resentful and discouraged. Guilt can keep a Christian from experiencing the abundant life Jesus desires for them.

❖ Focusing on God's Word

(About 20 Minutes)

Read aloud the introductory paragraph. Emphasize that we are unable to live up to the expectations of others or of God. Have a volunteer read aloud **Hebrews 10:1–2**. Then with pen in hand discuss the questions that follow.

1. Participants probably will underline "the same sacrifices repeated endlessly year after year." The sacrifice had to be repeated because it was never fully able to remove the load of guilt.

2. Jesus was the once for all sacrifice for sin. No longer do people have to burden themselves with a load of guilt.

3. The one-time sacrifice of Jesus took place on the cross.

4. Satan is the accuser. He accuses us by trying to convince us that Jesus' sacrifice wasn't enough, that we have to do something to earn forgiveness, that our sins are too great for Jesus to forgive, etc.

5. God desires that we live without guilt. He wants us to prosper and have a future filled with hope.

❖ Focusing on My Life

(About 10 Minutes)

1. Answers will vary. If comfortable doing so, allow time for volunteers to share specific ways Satan accuses.

❖

2. Allow time for each participant to complete this activiy.

❖ Focusing on the Week Ahead

(About 5 Minutes)

Urge participants to complete one or both of the activities before the next session. If time permits, provide participants with cards on which to write the Scripture references. Point out that the Holy Spirit will work through God's Word, strengthening their faith and enabling them to fight the accuser's attacks.

2—Guilt—
Can't Live with It, Can't Live without It

❖ Focusing Our Sights

(About 2 Minutes)

Read aloud this paragraph. Discuss briefly the questions.

❖ Focusing Our Attention

(About 10 Minutes)

Read the introductory paragraph in this section and give the group time to complete the two questions on their own. If they seem to have trouble with a question, use personal examples from your own life to help them get started.

❖ Focusing on the Issue

(About 10 Minutes)

Divide into four groups or have participants complete all sections. Discuss each of the four ways people usually deal with guilt. Allow those who feel comfortable doing so to share their reaction to the statements along with personal statements concerning times they have dealt with guilt in the manner described.

❖

❖ Focusing on God's Word

(About 10 Minutes)

Read the questions aloud and answer them together.

1. Jesus (a perfect, sinless man) sacrificed Himself by dying on the cross for us.

2. Jesus Christ provides the answer for the hurt of our guilt. When we confess our sins to Him, He heals us, removes our guilt, and restores our relationship to God.

3. We are all sinners. Guilt is like gravity. You can deny its existence, but it doesn't take away the fact that it exists.

4. Others may try to use guilt to get us to do what they desire, or we may try to use guilt on others as well. When we do this, or it is done to us, we put ourselves and others back under the condemnation of the Law, that from which Jesus Christ freed us. It may have a temporary short-term gain, but it doesn't work over the long haul.

5. The inability to forgive ourselves can leave us living under the weight of all our guilt. Instead of living in the freedom of Christ's love, guilt can cause us to live as unbelievers.

6. We must take responsibility for our actions. As long as we point to others as the cause of our problems, we remain locked in the past and unable to experience the joy of God's forgiveness for others and ourselves.

❖ Focusing on My Life

(About 10 Minutes)

Read the instructions and provide quiet time for the participants to reflect and complete this activity in pairs. Read the closing prayer together.

❖ Focusing on the Week Ahead

(About 2 Minutes)

Urge participants to consider the suggestions in thissection before the next session

3—Guilt
and the Hardened Heart

❖ Focusing Our Sights

(About 1 Minute)

Read aloud or have a volunteer read aloud the opening paragraph.

❖ Focusing Our Attention

(About 10 Minutes)

Read aloud the opening paragraph. Give volunteers the opportunity to react to the woman's statement. Introduce Corrie ten Boom and the story of her meeting with a former Nazi guard. Then have volunteers read portions of the long quote. Discuss the questions that follow.

1. Corrie may have experienced anger, hatred, bitterness, resentment, self-pity, etc.

2. The former guard probably wondered if she would accept him and forgive him once she knew the truth about his past.

3. Answers will vary.

❖ Focusing on the Issue

(About 10 Minutes)

1. (a) Corrie's relationship with God would be strained since she rejected His command to love others. (b) If she does not forgive, her anger might consume her. (c) She will focus on all the terrible things he had done.

2. The former guard needed to know whether Corrie's words about the power of God's forgiveness were genuine and true.

3. Corrie recognizes that all people are sinners. Like the former Nazi guard, Corrie acknowledges that she also needs God's forgiveness.

Have volunteers read aloud the conclusion to the story.

4. When Corrie forgave the former guard she gave up revenge, pity, and hatred toward him.

5. The Holy Spirit enabled Corrie to forgive the former guard.

6. The former guard then needed to seize God's forgiveness and forgive himself.

❖ Focusing on God's Word

(About 10 Minutes)

Read aloud the opening paragraph. Then ask for volunteers to read aloud **Colossians 3:12–17.**

1. Participants will have circled *compassion, kindness, humility, gentleness, patience, love,* and *gratitude.*

2. Participants will have underlined *Bear with each other and forgive whatever grievances you have against one another. Forgive as the Lord forgave you.*

3. Participants will have drawn a box around *Let the peace of Christ rule in your hearts* and *Let the word of Christ dwell in you richly.*

4. God works forgiveness as we confess our sins to Him.

5. Through confession we receive personal assurance of God's forgiveness through faith in Jesus.

❖ Focusing on My Life

(About 10 Minutes)

1. Answers will vary. Some of the results of unforgiveness include vengeance, hatred, anger, jealousy, and rage.

2–3. Answers will vary. Allow volunteers to share.

Have a volunteer read aloud the sponge analogy. Discuss the question that follows.

4. God's love and forgiveness softens our hearts and enables us to forgive others.

Pray together the prayer. Remind participants that God's great love for us empowers us to love others.

❖ Focusing on the Week Ahead

(About 2 Minutes)

Urge participants to make an appointment with the pastor for private confession.

Read aloud or have a volunteer read aloud the story Corrie ten Boom tells about a time when she had trouble forgetting a situation for which she had forgiven someone. Discuss with participants.

4—Encouraging One Another—Freedom from Guilt

❖ Focusing Our Sights

Read aloud the opening paragraph.

❖ Focusing Our Attention

(About 10 Minutes)
Read the five statements listed in this section.

❖ Focusing on the Issue

(About 10 Minutes)
1. They are all discouraging. They cause the people to whom they are addressed to feel guilty.

2. Answers will vary.

3–5. Allow time for the group members to complete these privately. When all are finished, if you choose, share your answers with the group and invite them to do the same.

❖ Focusing on God's Word

(About 15 Minutes)
Ask for a volunteer to read the passage to the group. Answer the questions together.

1. Jesus' death on the cross took away our barrier to God, our sins, giving us complete and unlimited access to Him.

2. Because Jesus shed His blood for us, we can *draw near to God with a clear conscience,* having our hearts sprinkled to *cleanse us from our guilty conscience.*

3 (a) Draw nearer to God.

(b) Hold unswervingly to the hope we profess.

(c) Spur one another on toward love and good deeds.

(d) Don't give up meeting together.

(e) Encourage one another.

4. All five could be torpedoed by discouraging statements from others or, at the very least, cause a believer to have greater difficulty following the path God has led him or her to follow.

5 (a) Sometimes I have felt far away from God too, but I am reassured that He promises never to leave me or forsake me.

(b) God promises to be with us in whatever we go through. He will see you through this.

(c) I really appreciate the fact that you did all this work. Things wouldn't have gone as well as they did without the work you did beforehand.

(d) I've missed seeing you at church lately. Is there anything troubling you that I can help with?

❖ Focusing on My Life

(About 15 Minutes)

1–2. Answers will vary.

3. Jesus accepted and loved us while we were still sinners.

4. God's love for us in Jesus enables to love others. Urge participants to list specific ways in which they can demonstrate God's love to others.

5. As we accept others, we are able to demonstrate love and encouragement. God's love transforms lives. His love provides a spirit of cooperation and love, acceptance and good will.

❖

6. Complete ~~the activity~~

7. Pray toge~~ther~~ ~~ac~~tivity.

❖ Focusing on the Week Ahead

(About 2 Minutes)

Urge participants to complete one or both activities during the coming week.

56

❖